Ana and Pip

by Angela Báez • illustrated by Brenda Figueroa

Lucy Calkins and Michael Rae-Grant, Series Editors

LETTER-SOUND CORRESPONDENCES
m, t, a, n, s, ss, p, i, d, g, o, c, k, ck, r, u

HIGH-FREQUENCY WORDS
is, like, see, the, no, so

Ana and Pip
Author: Angela Báez
Series Editors: Lucy Calkins and Michael Rae-Grant

Heinemann
145 Maplewood Avenue, Suite 300
Portsmouth, NH 03801
www.heinemann.com

Cataloging-in-Publication data is on file with the Library of Congress.

ISBN-13: 978-0-325-13798-8

Design and Production: Dinardo Design LLC, Carole Berg, and Rebecca Anderson

Editors: Anna Cockerille and Jennifer McKenna

Illustrations: Brenda Figueroa

Photograph: p. 32 © aceshot1/Shutterstock

Manufacturing: Gerard Clancy

Printed in the United States of America on acid-free paper
2 3 4 5 6 7 8 9 10 MP 28 27 26 25 24 23 22
November 2022 Printing / PO# 34910

Contents

Meet...
Ana
Pip
Dad
Abuela

Is Pip Up?

The sun is up.

I am up.

Dad is up.

Is Pip up?

No, Pip is not up.
Pip is on the rug.

I sip the cup,

and Dad sips the mug.

Is Pip up?
Pip?

No, Pip is not up.
Pip is on the pack.

I tug and tug on the pack.

UG!

I must run, and

Pip is not up.

So I am sad.

I miss Pip.

Pat,
pat,
pat.
Pat,
pat,
pat.

Dad, Pip is up!

I see Pip in the window!

I like Pip!
And Pip likes Ana!

2

Pip Is Not It!

Dad, Pip, and I
play tag.

Dad sits.

I run, and Pip runs.

Dad runs and
runs and . . . tag!

I see Pip.

So I run and run and . . . tag!

Pip runs and runs and...

UG!

Pip is stuck in the mud,

so Pip can’t run.

Dad sees Pip and
runs in the mud.

Dad digs and digs.

Dad tugs and tugs and...

Pip is not stuck!

And . . . tag!

Dad is it!

3

Abuela and the Drum

I can play the drum,
and Dad can play the drum.

Rat, tat . . . TAT!
Rat, tat . . . tat!
Rat, tat . . . tat!

STOP!

“Can Abuela play?” I ask.

Abuela nods.

I pick up sticks
and a can
and a top.

I rip and cut.
I tug and tuck.
It is a drum!

"Can Abuela play
the drum?" I ask.

Rat, tat.
Rat, tat.
TAT!

Rum, tum.
Rum, tum.
TUM!

Abuela CAN play the drum!

Learn about...

CATS

Many people have a pet cat, just like Ana. Pet cats are often soft, cuddly, and playful. Their fur can be orange like Pip's, or it can be black, brown, gray, tan, or white. Some cats have no fur at all—they're totally hairless!

Pet cats sleep a lot, as much as twenty hours in one day. But when cats *are* awake, they can be ferocious hunters. Cats are *carnivores*—they only eat meat—so their bodies are specially designed to help them hunt. They can sneak up and pounce on little animals they want to eat. *Pounce* means they jump on the animal really fast and catch it, super quick!

Because cats are carnivores, they have sharp claws and pointy teeth. But don't worry—pet cats usually only eat cat food, and usually only pounce on their toys.

Talk about...

Ask your reader some questions like...

- What happened in this book?
- Turn to page 8. Why was Ana feeling sad in this part?
- How did Ana make a drum for Abuela?
- Abuela has a special talent—she can play the drum! What special talents do people in your family have?